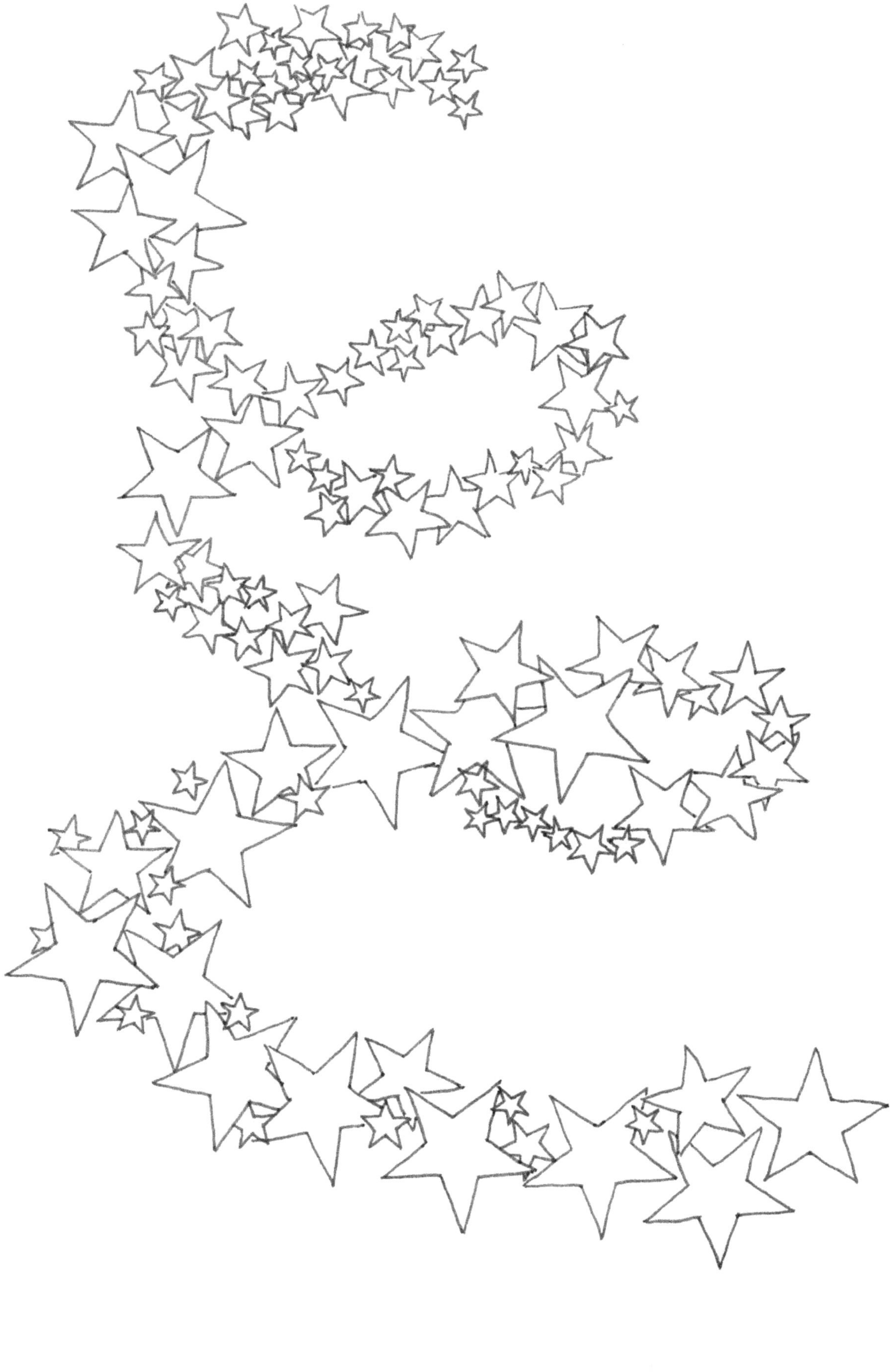

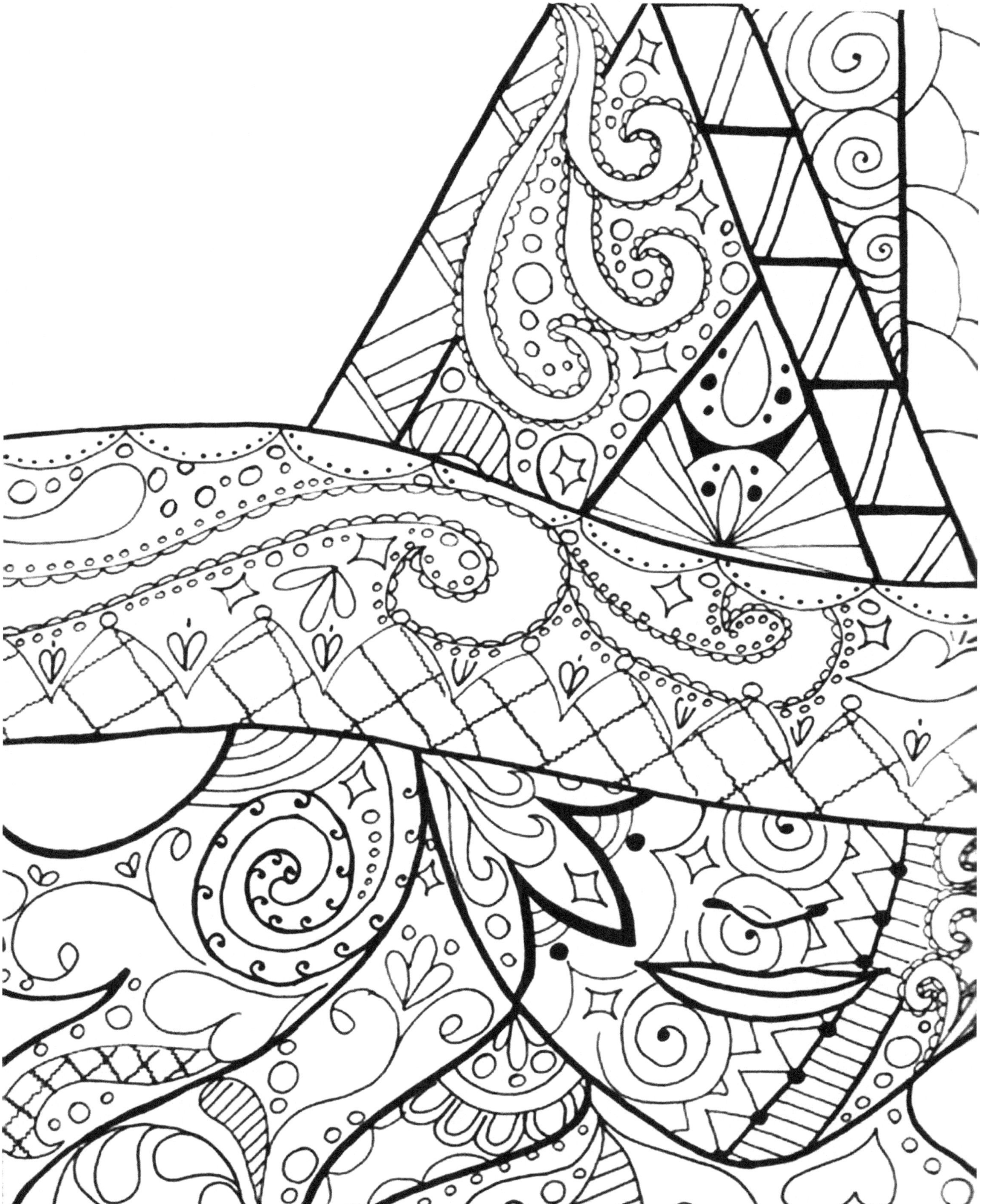

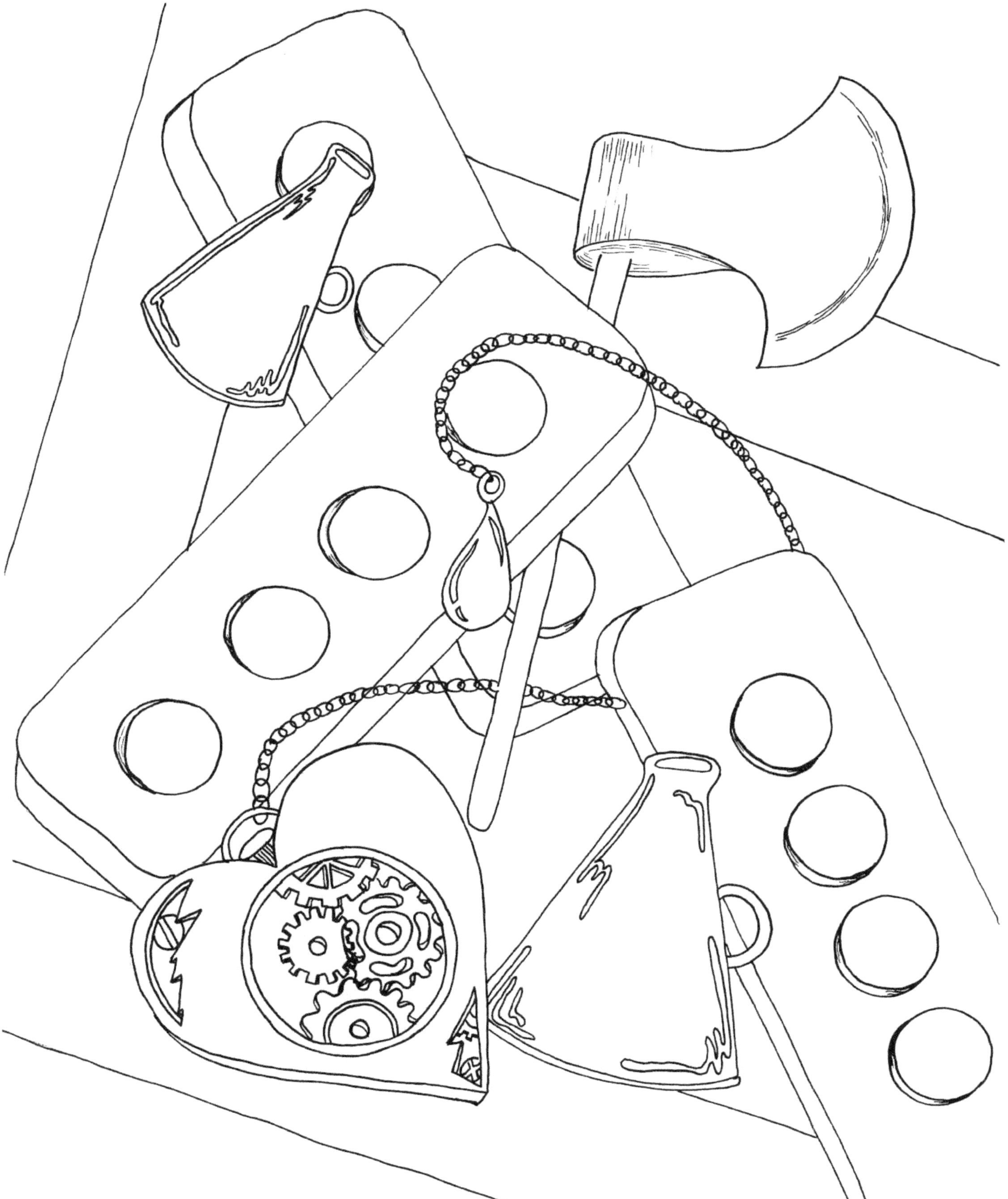

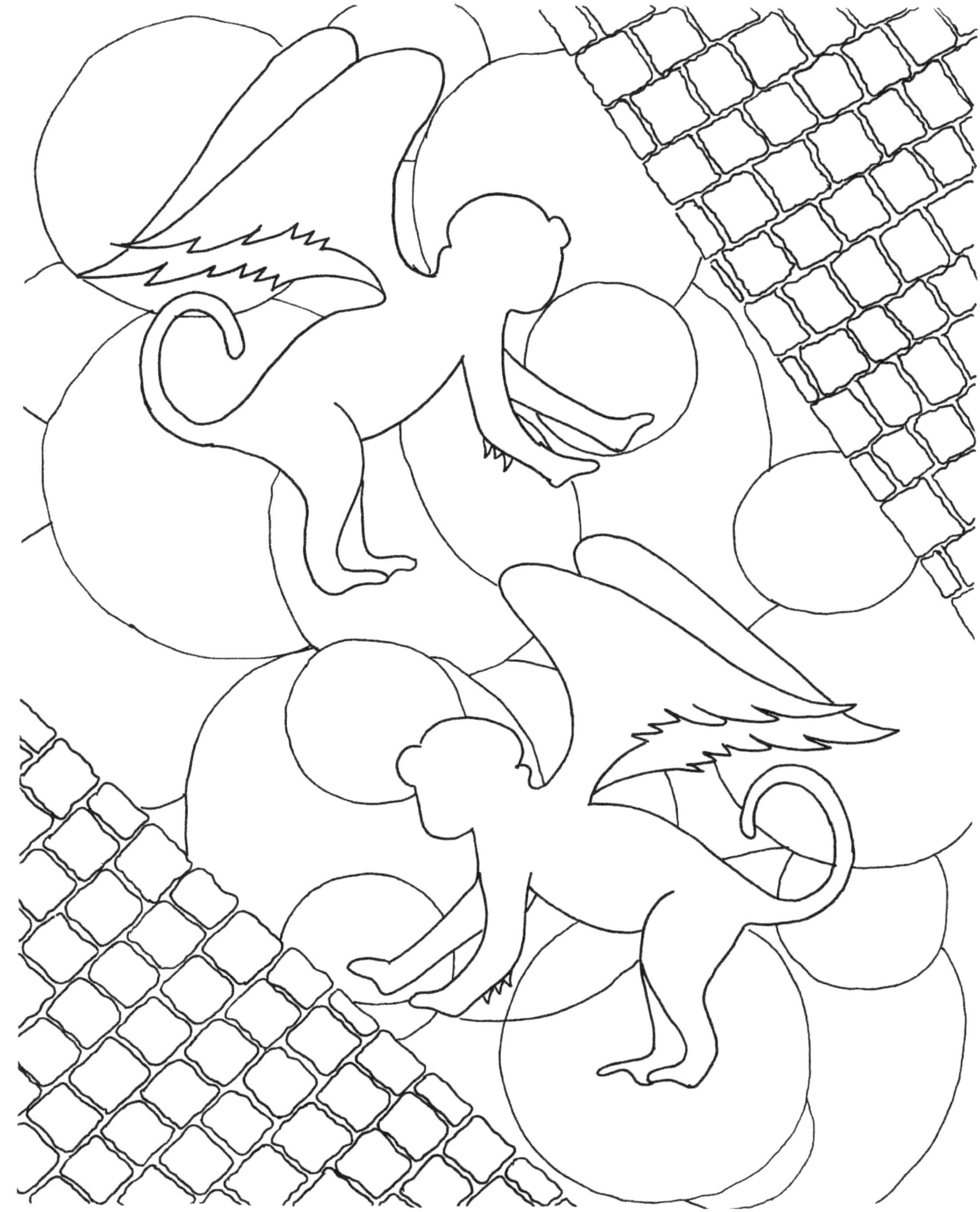

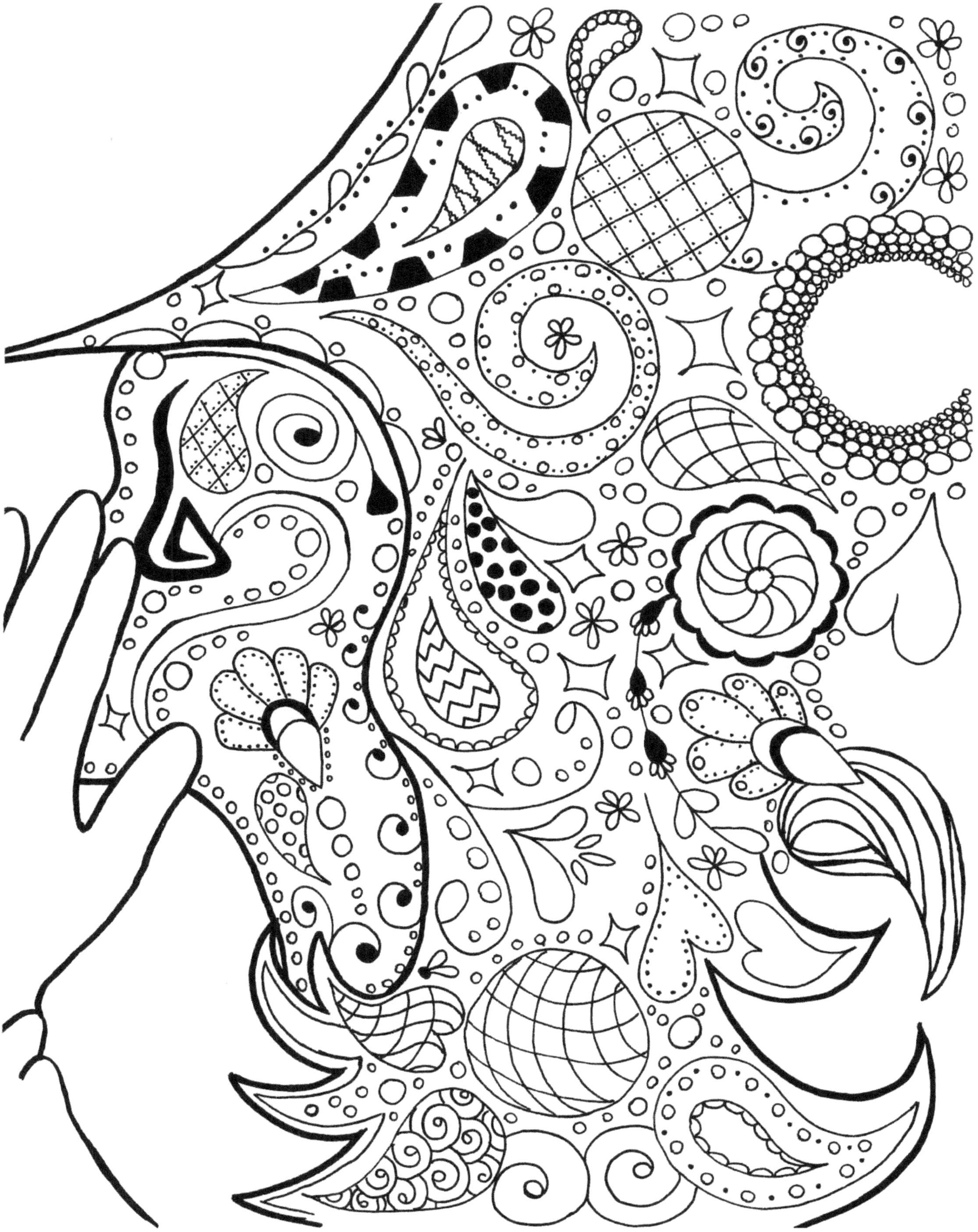

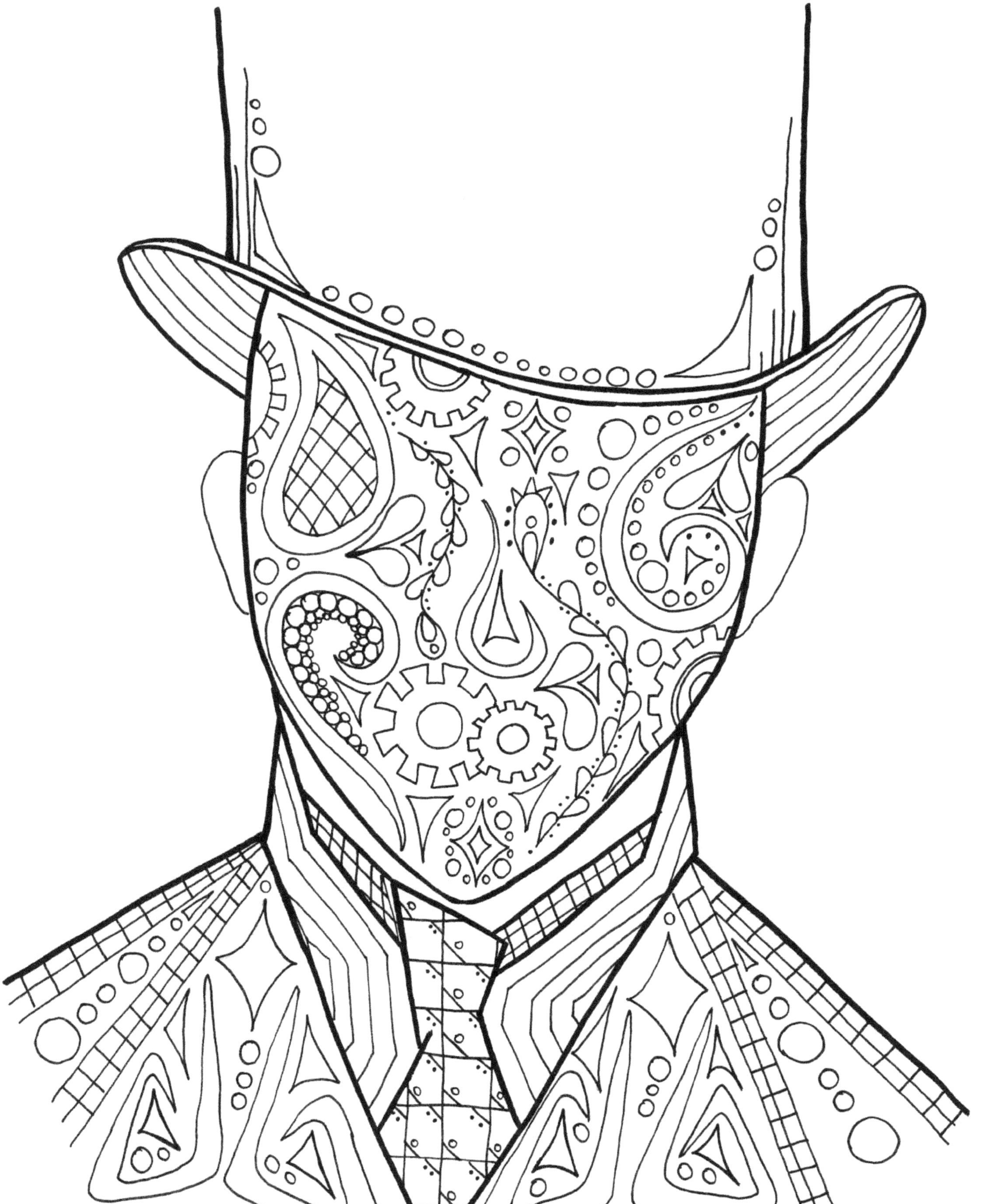

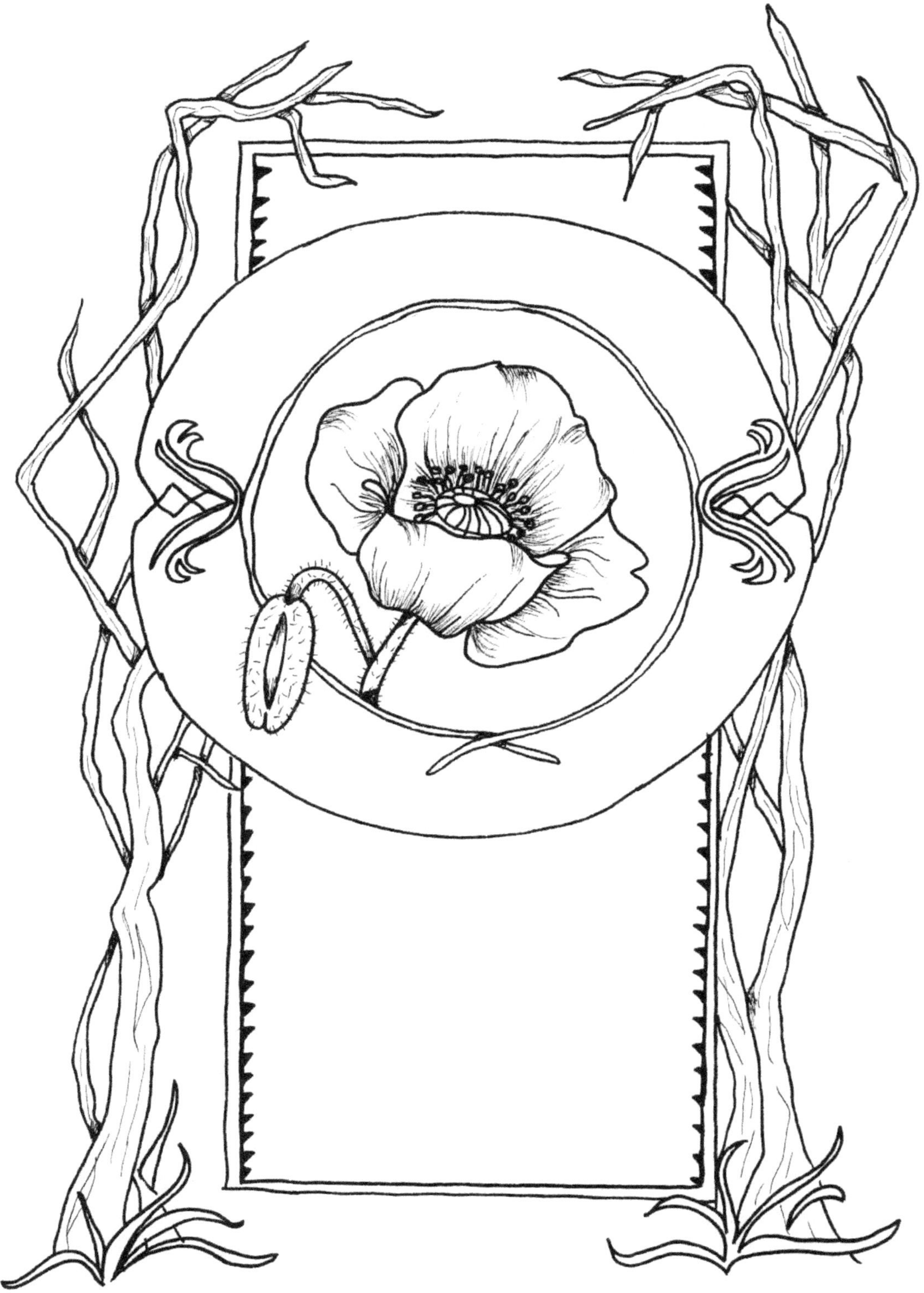

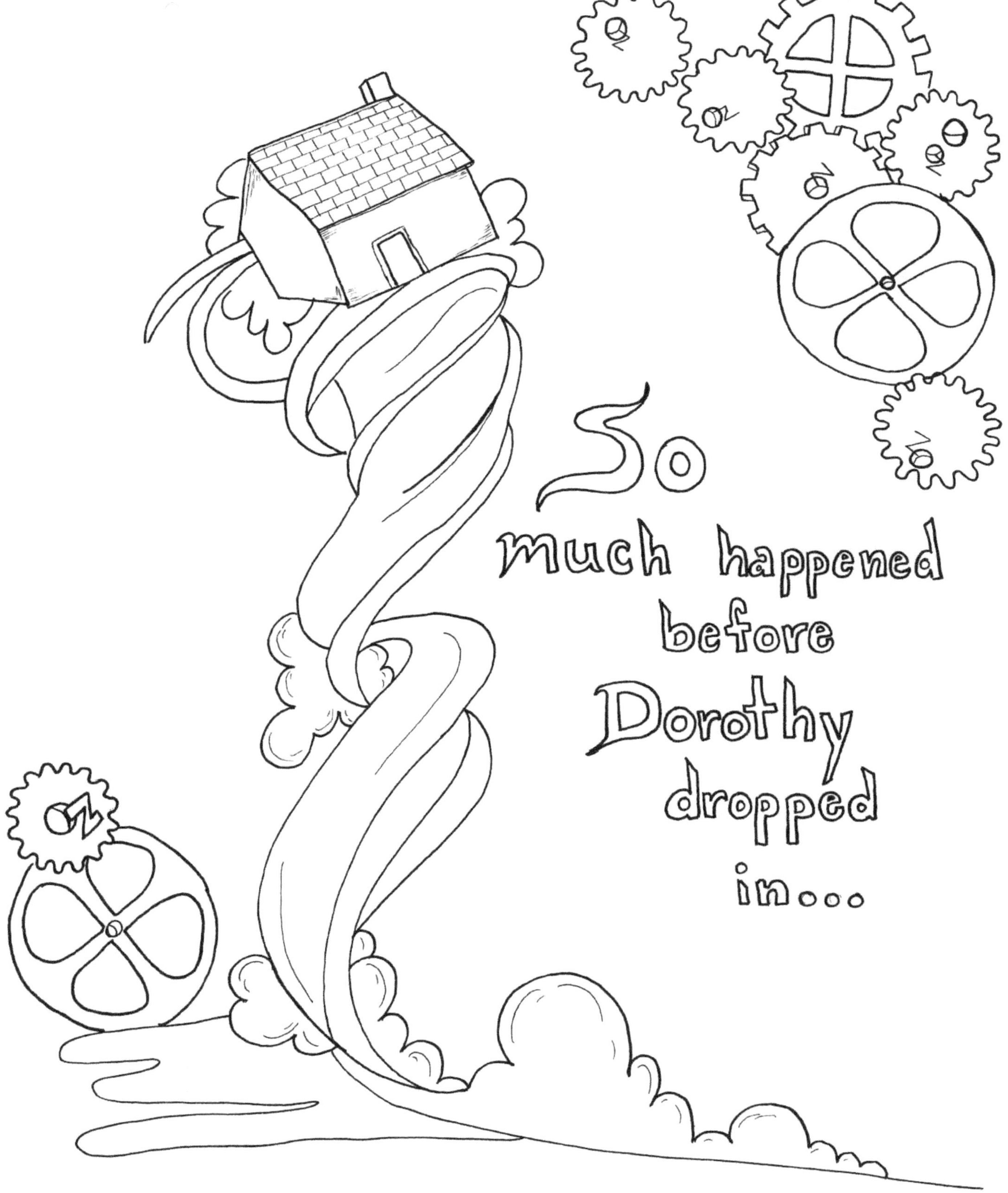
So
much happened
before
Dorothy
dropped
in...

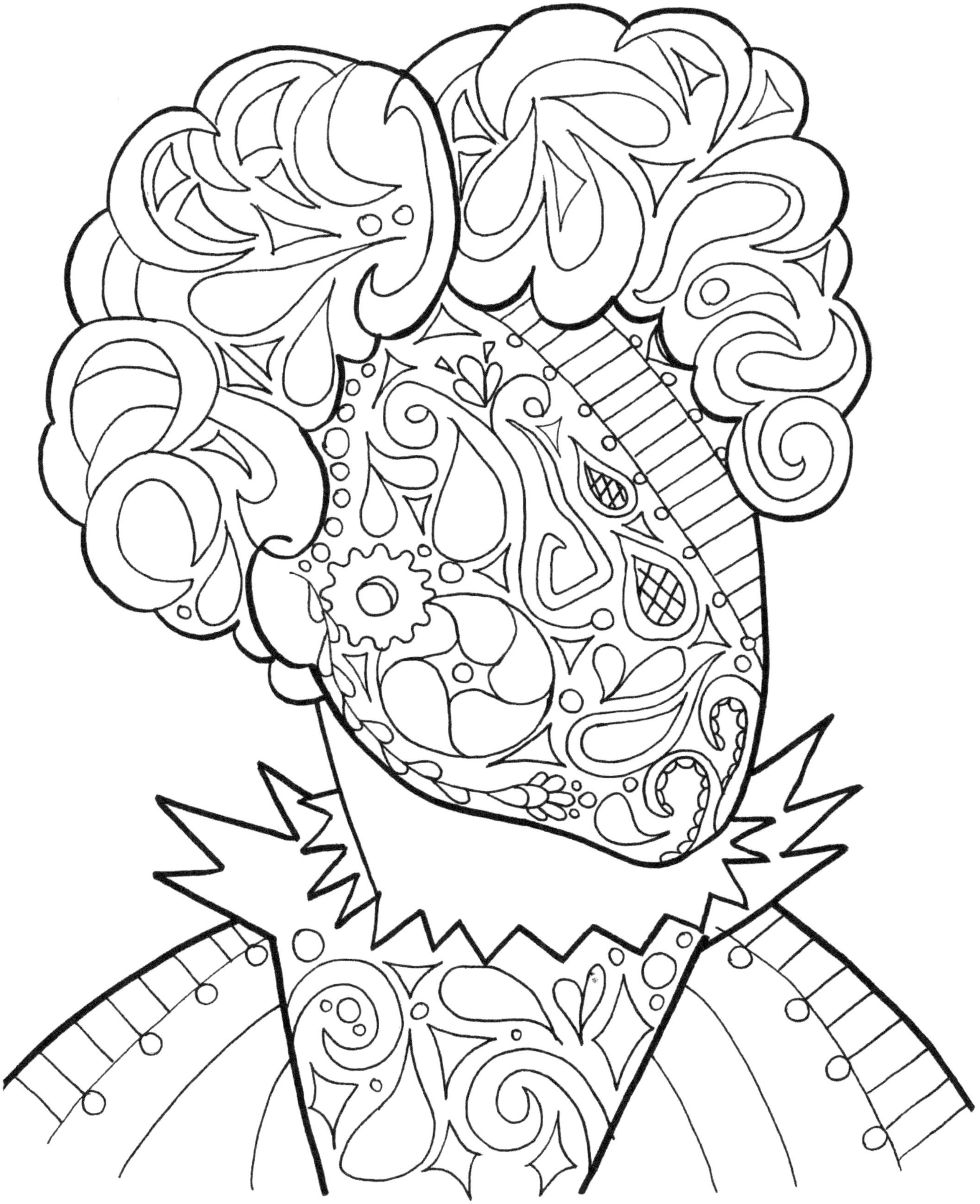

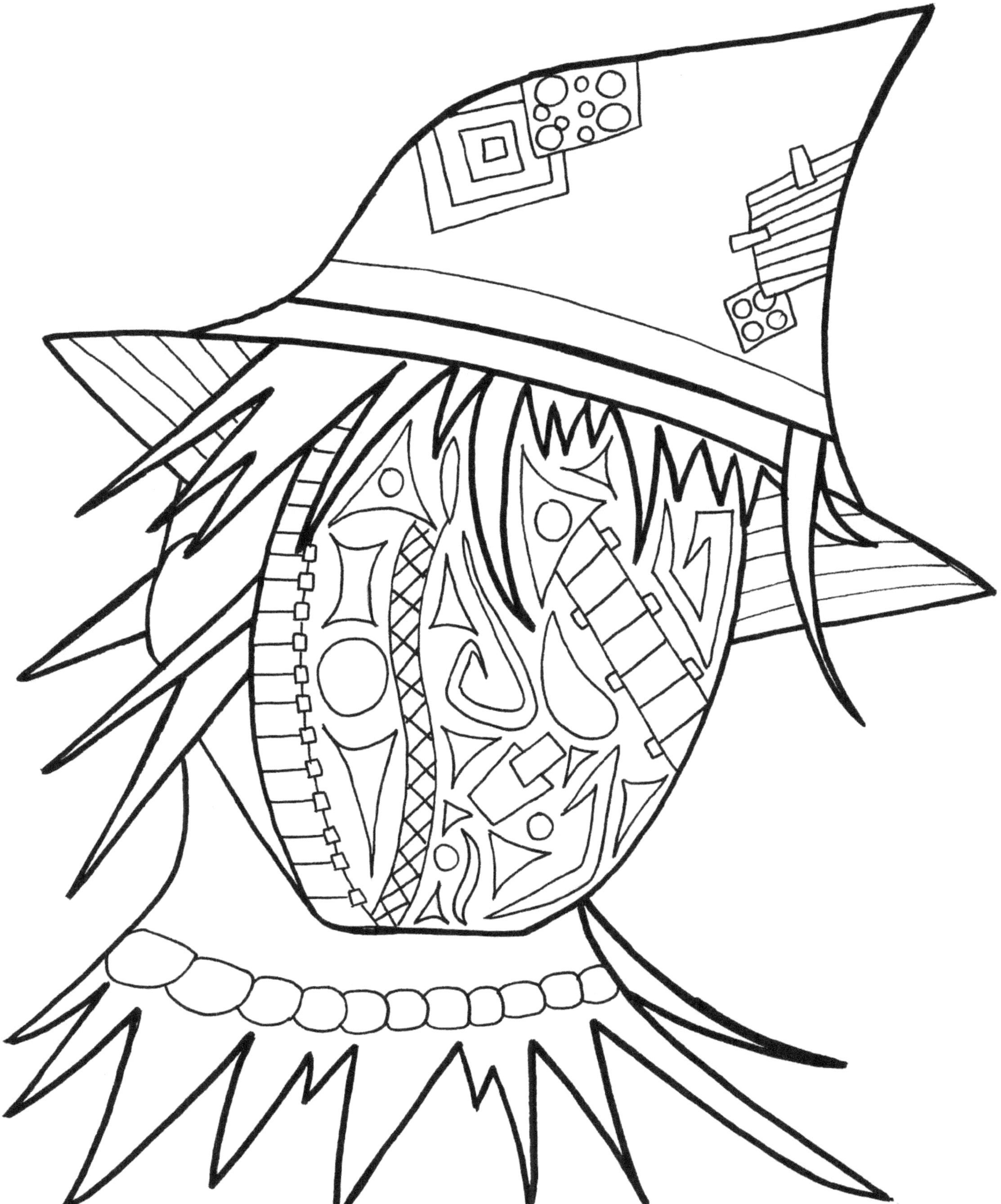

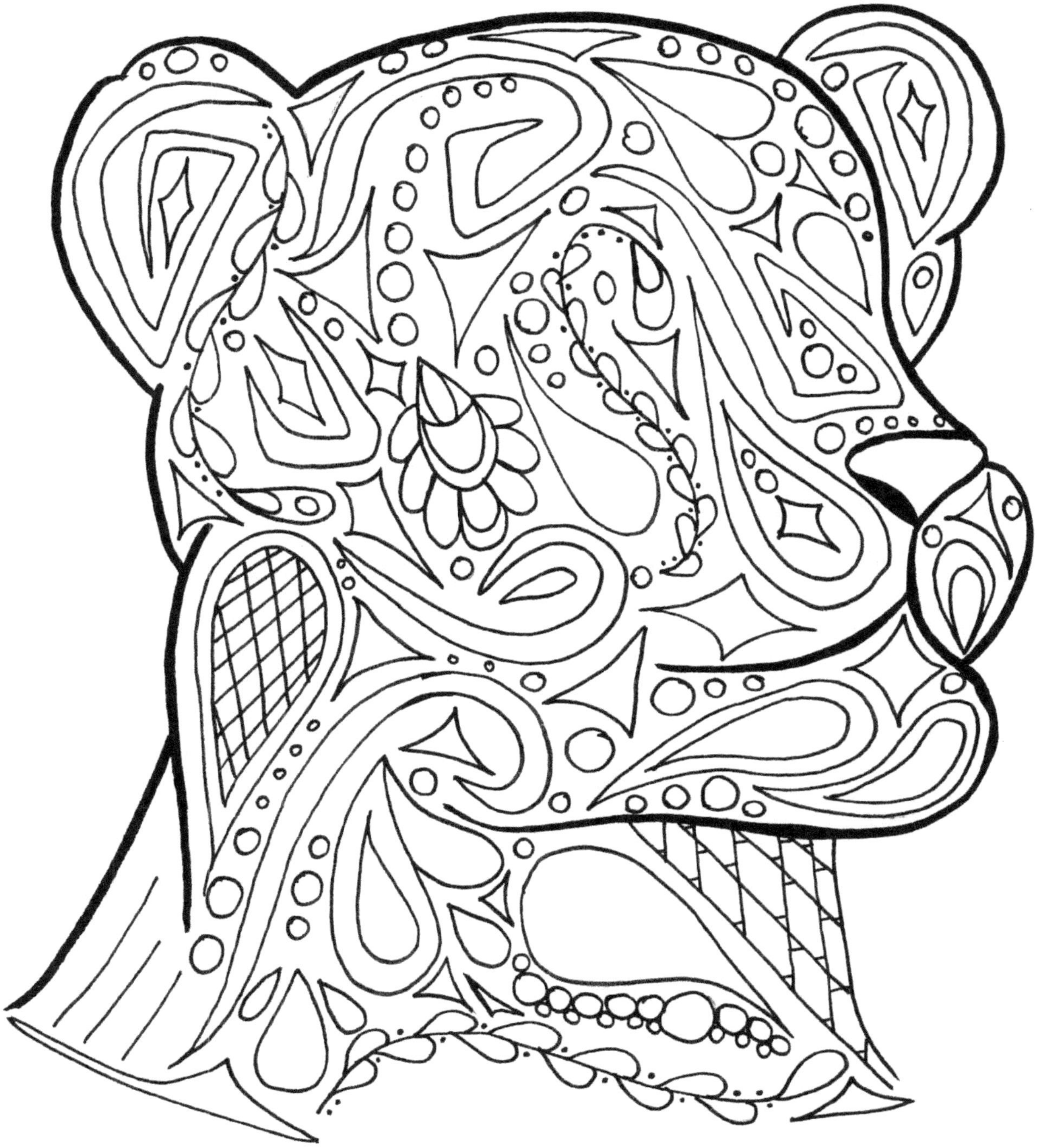

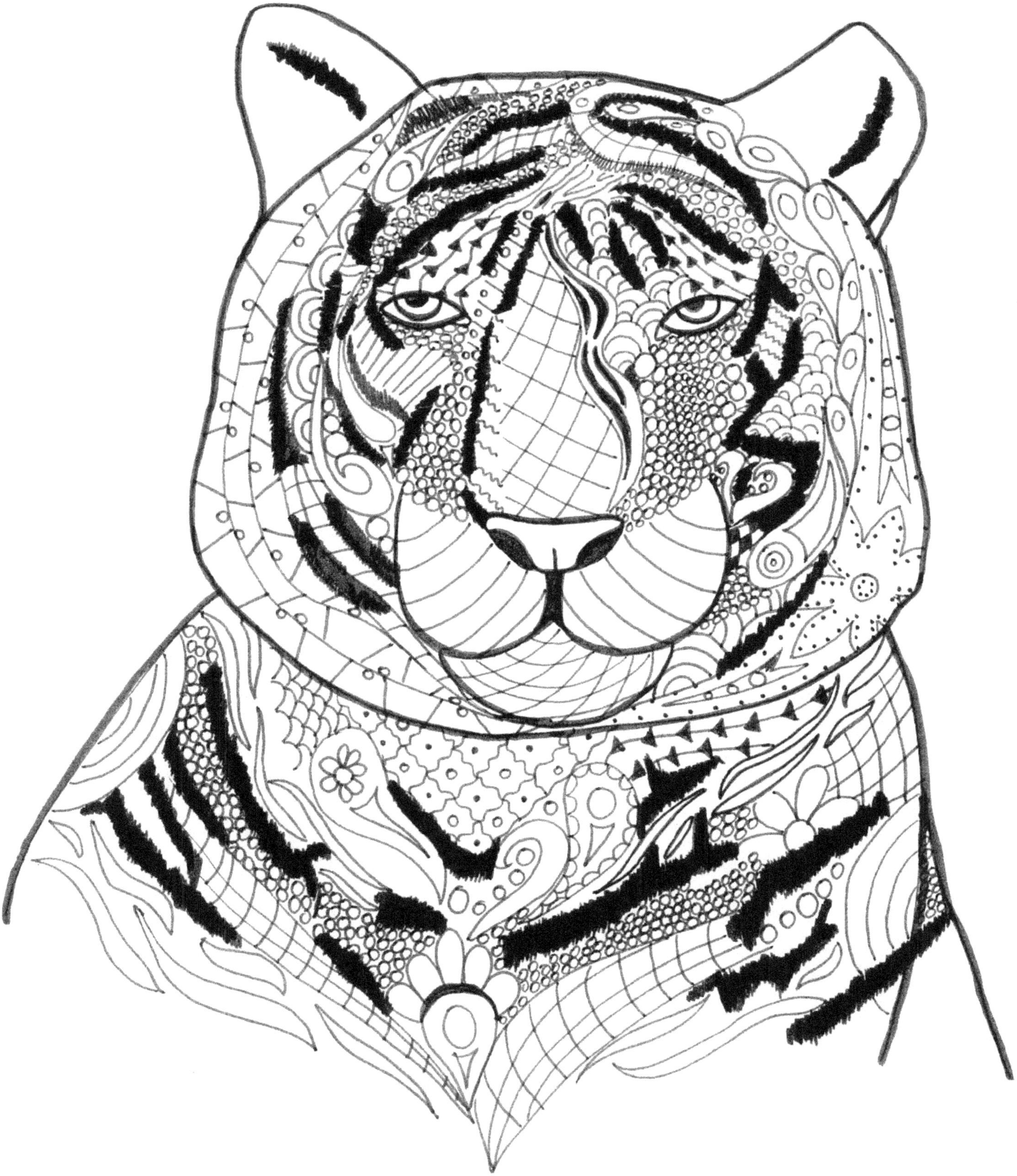

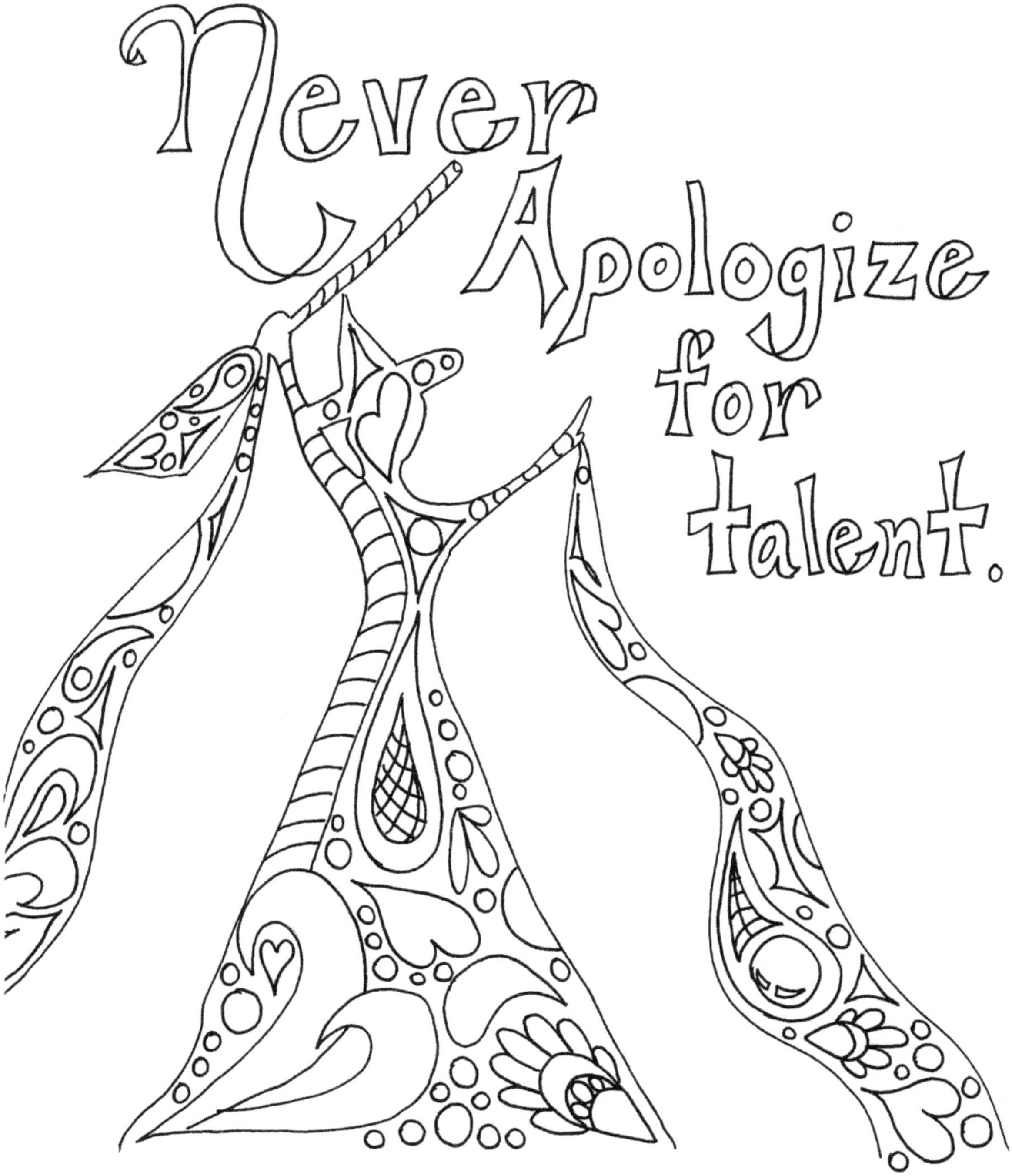
Never
Apologize
for
talent.

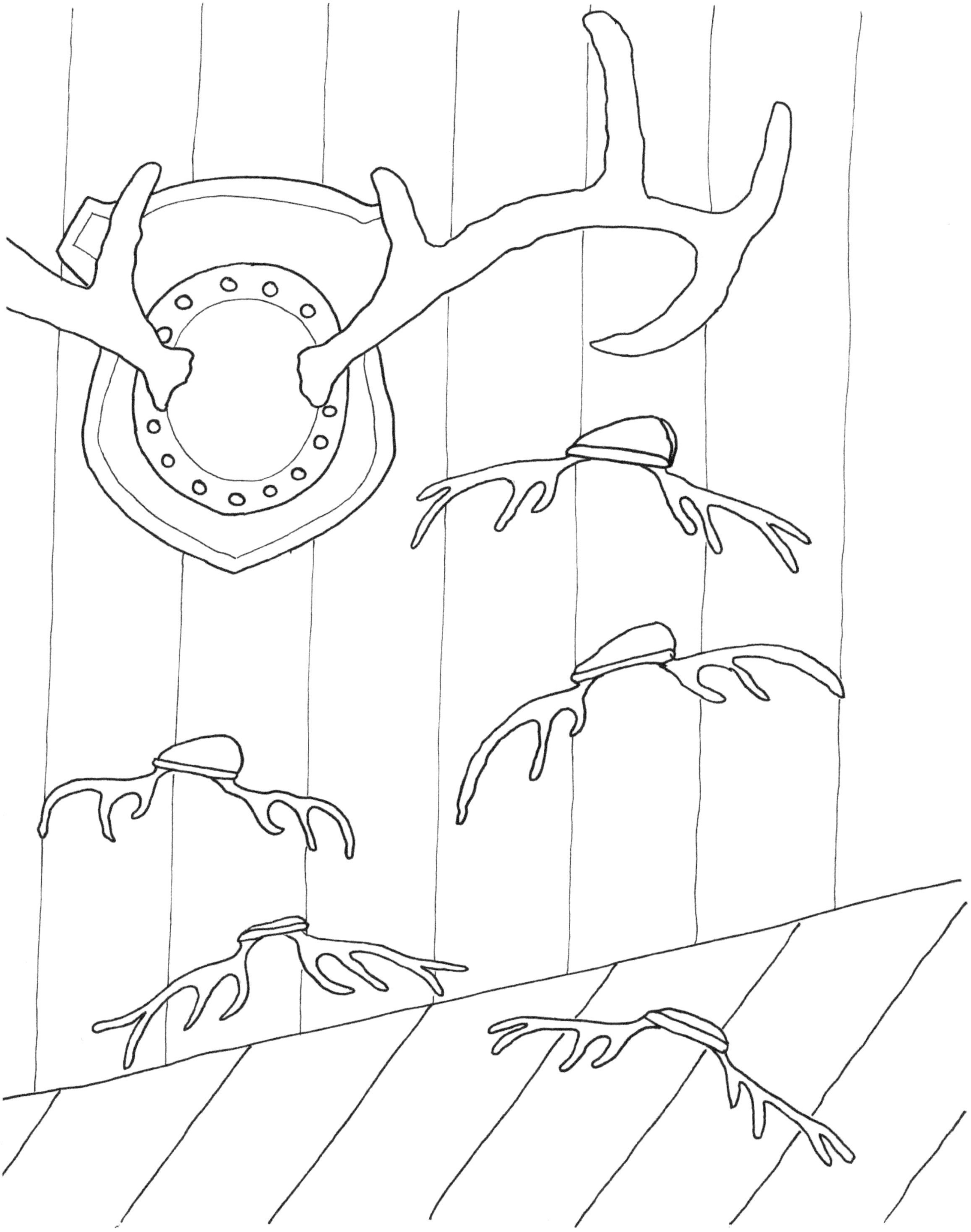

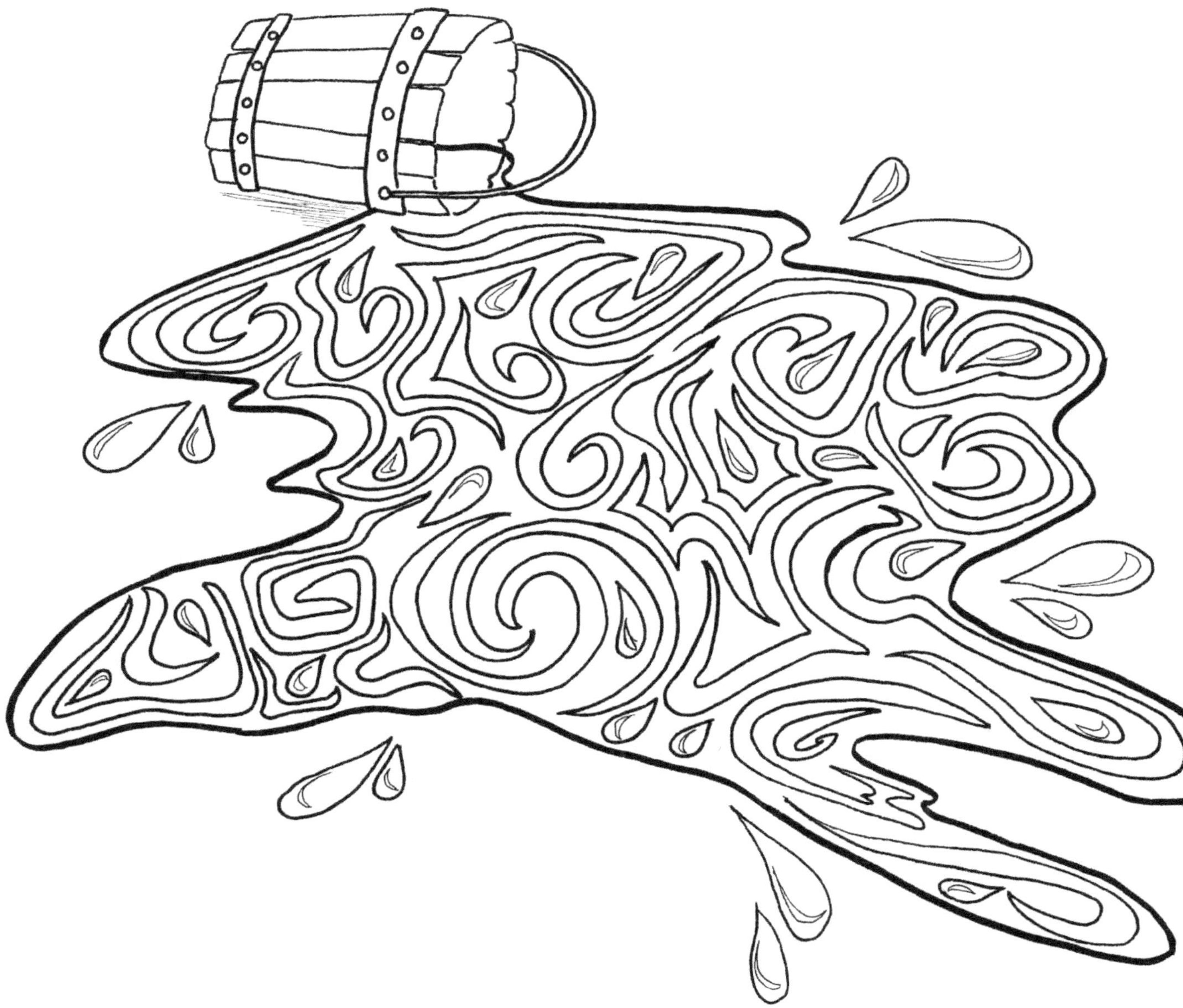

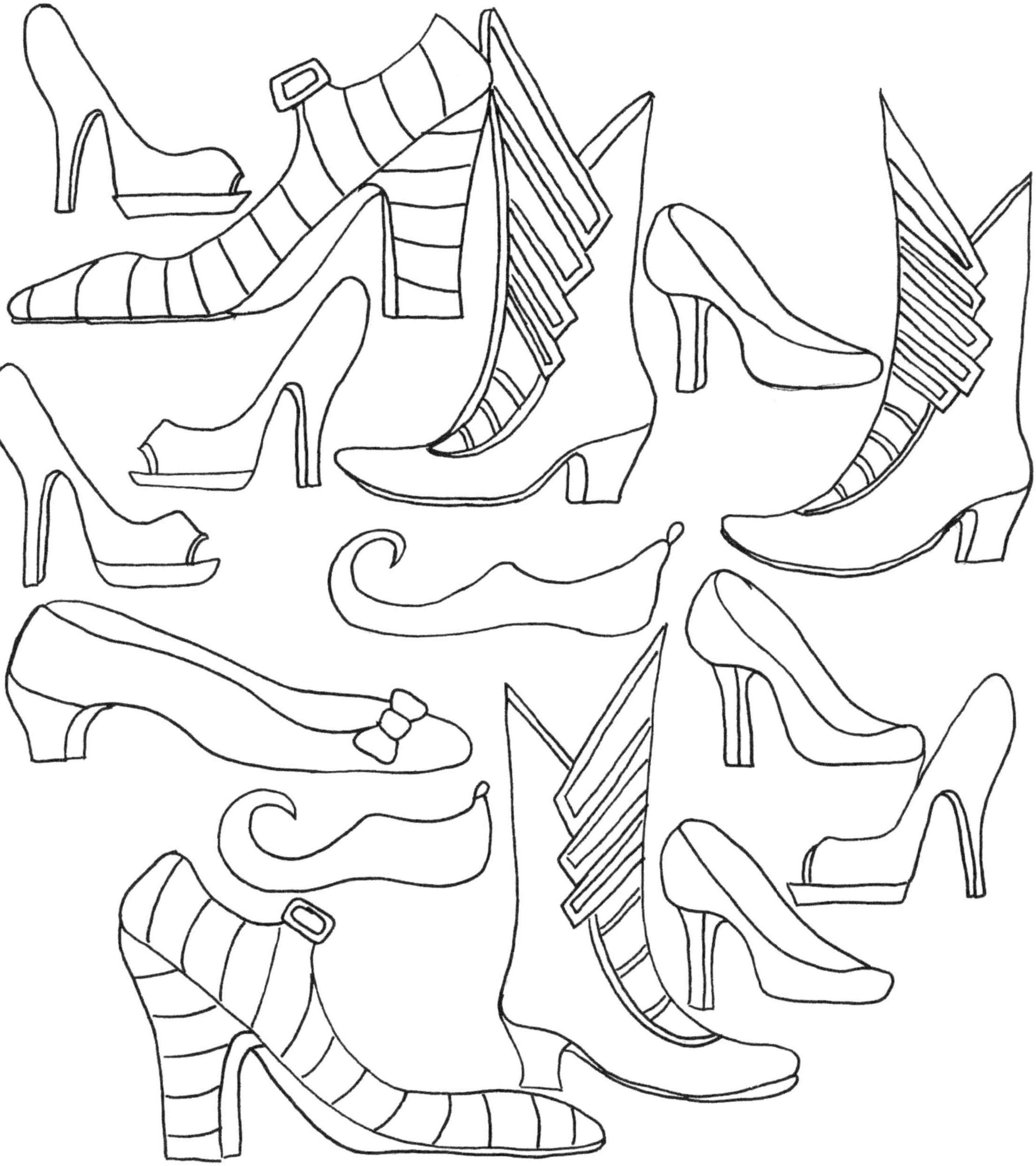

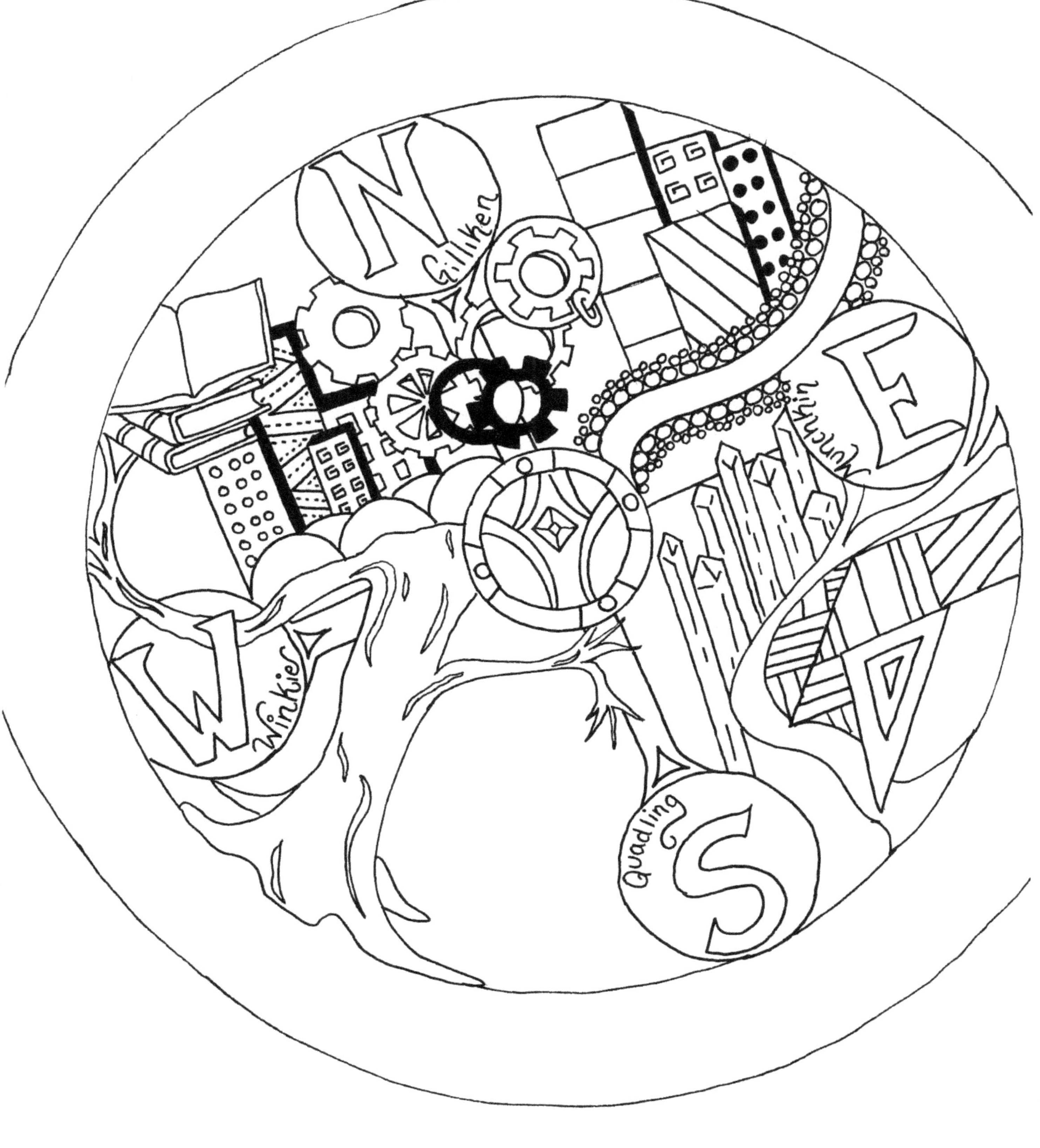
N
Gilliken
E
Munchkin
W
Winkies
S
Quadling

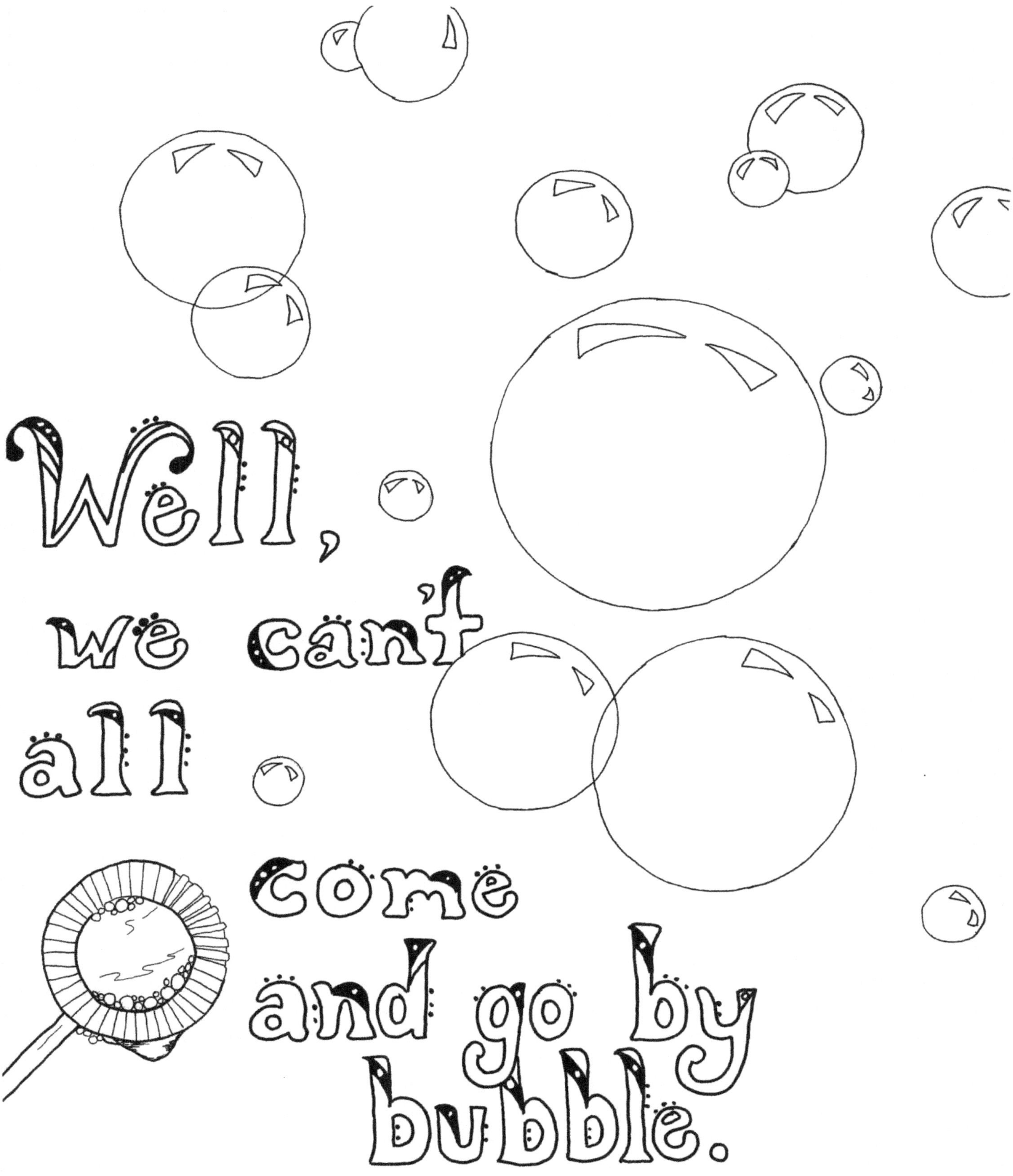
Well, we can't all come and go by bubble.

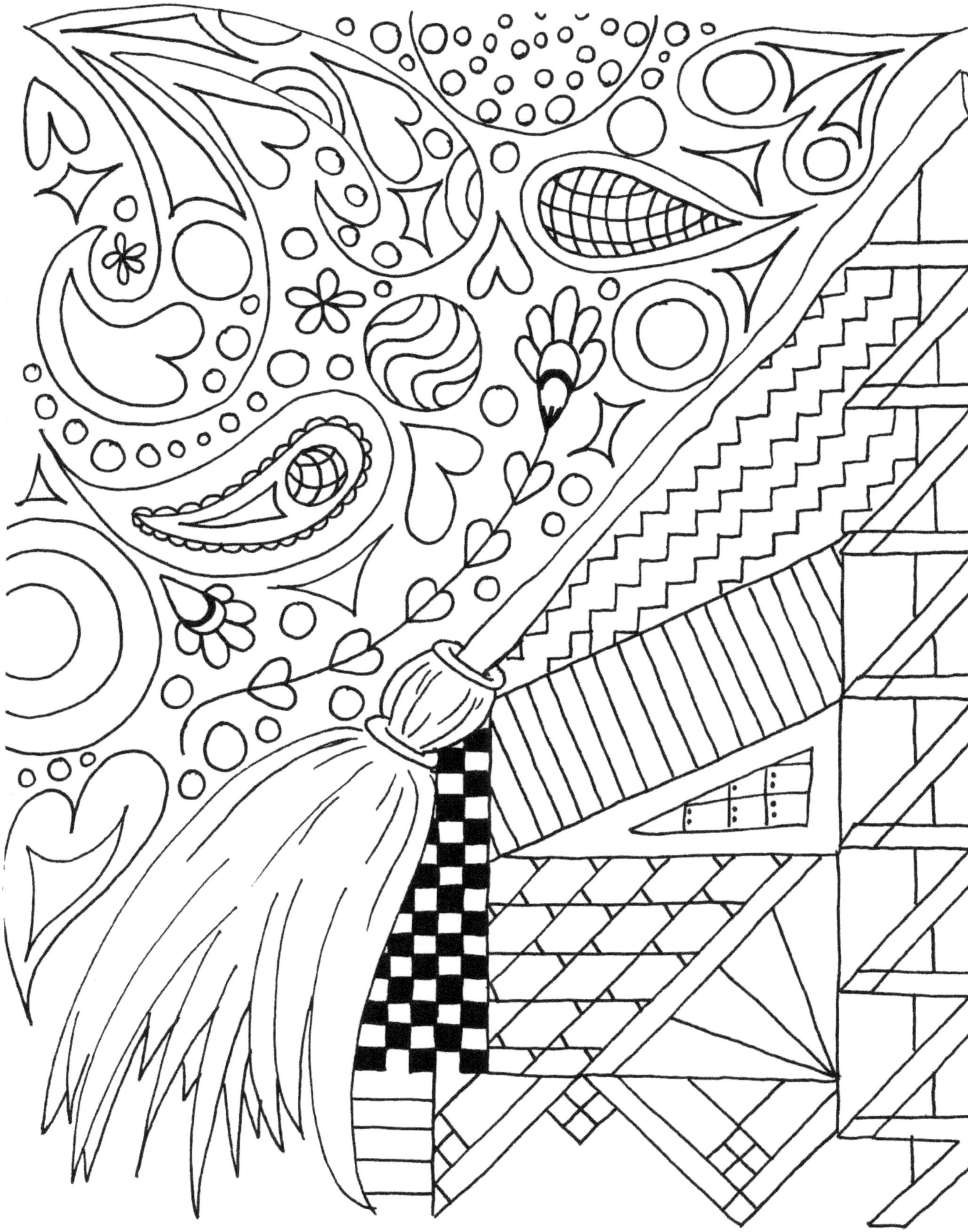

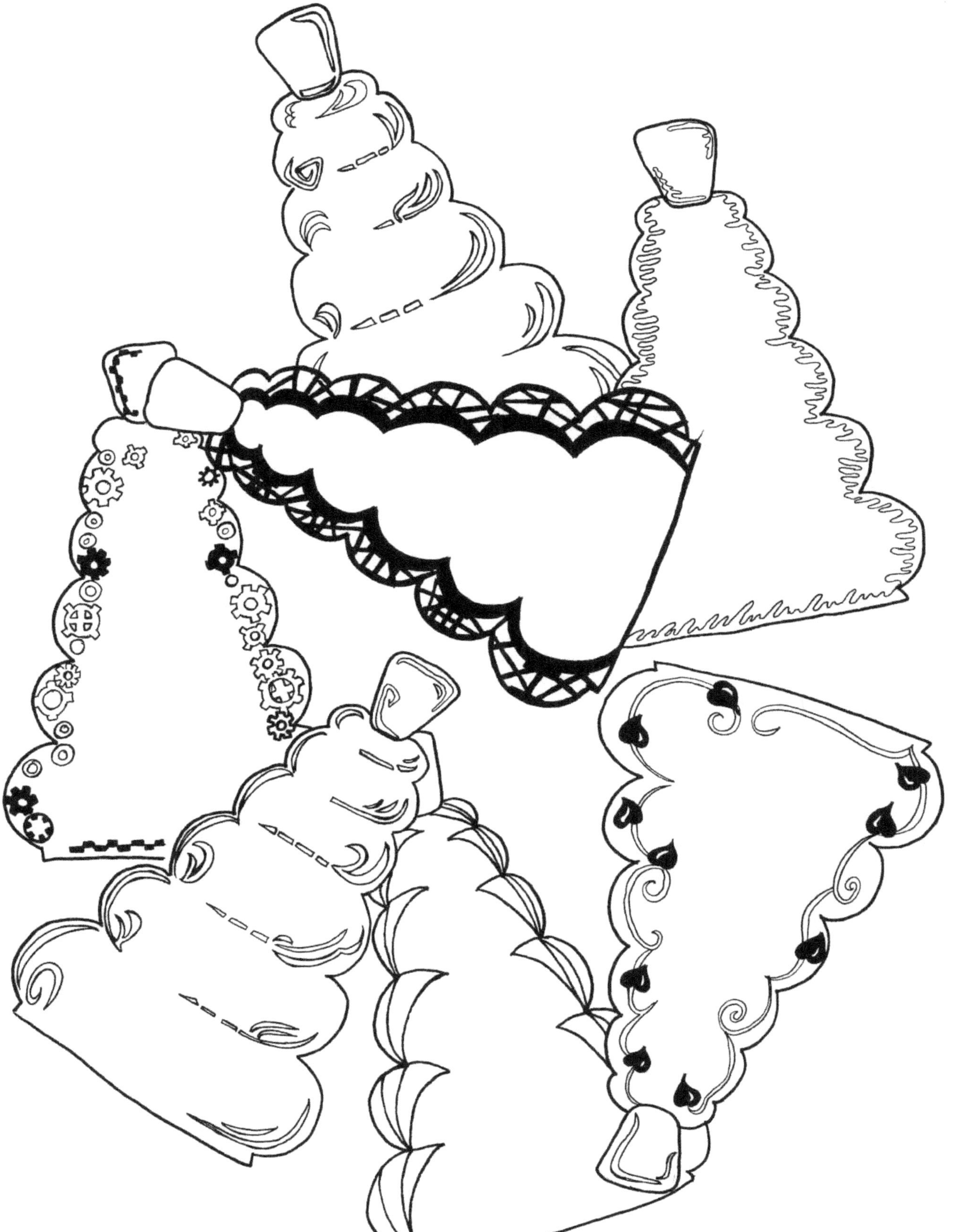

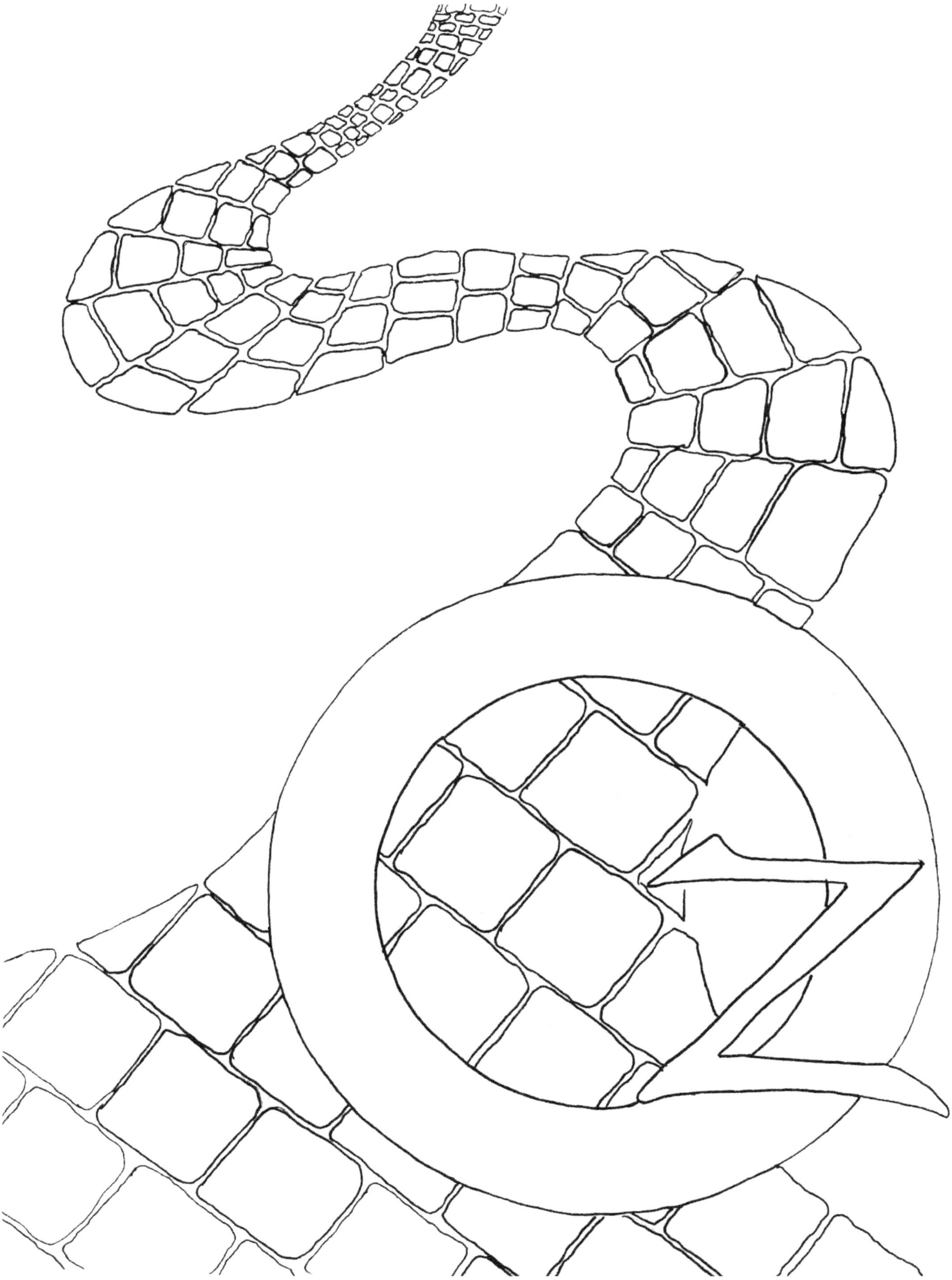

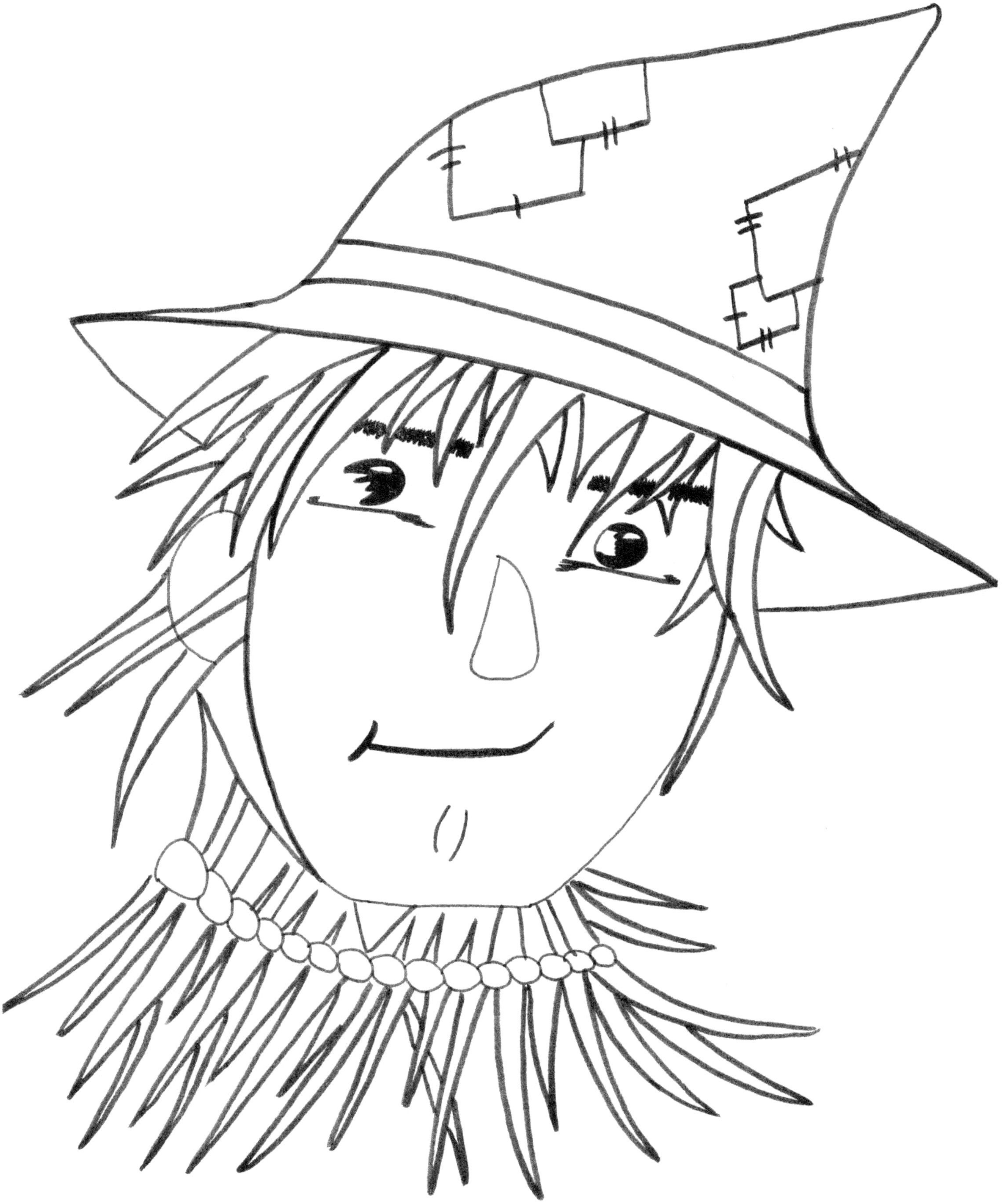

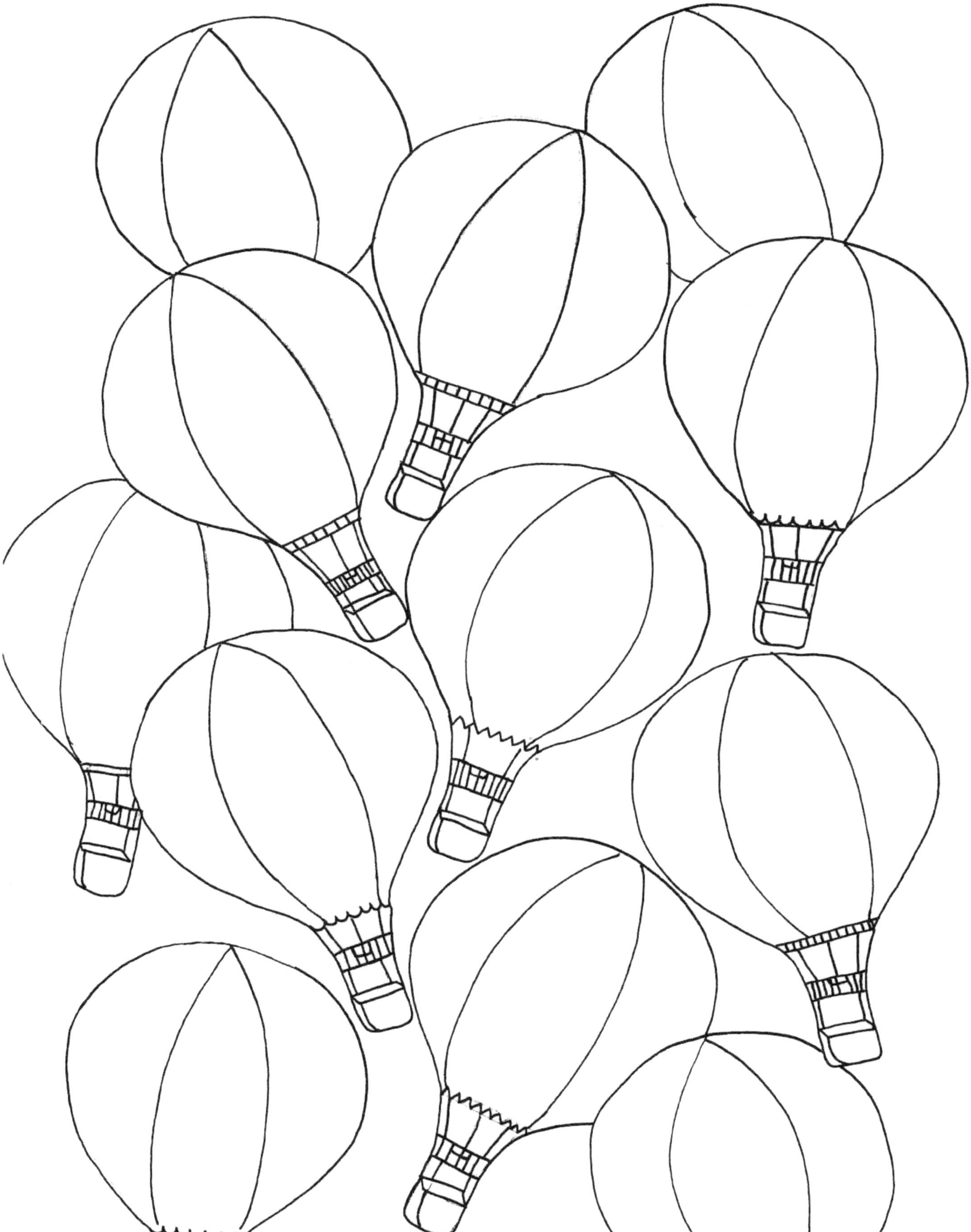

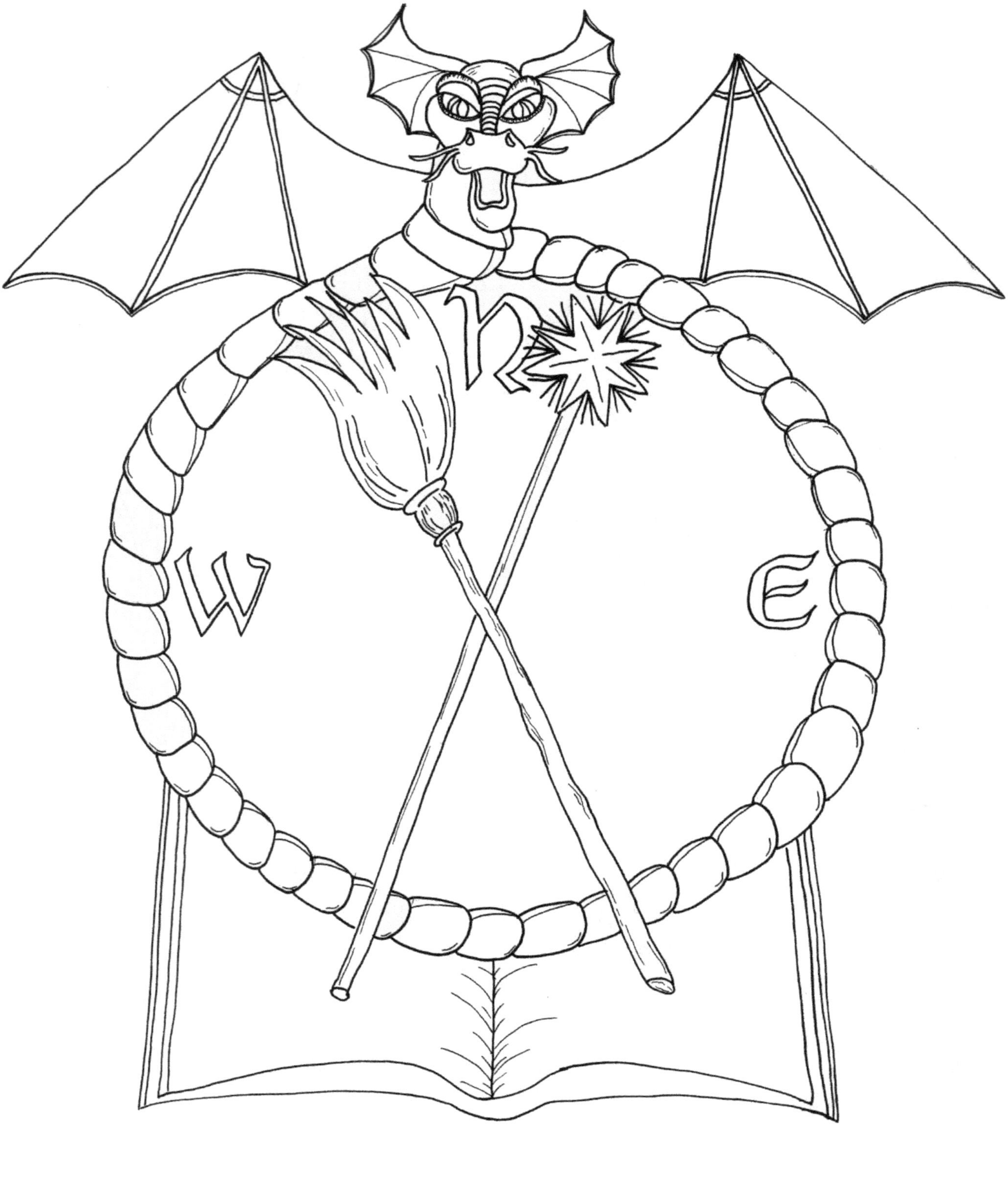
N
W
E

www.ingramcontent.com/pod-product-compliance
Lightning Source LLC
Chambersburg PA
CBHW080609190526
45169CB00007B/2945
9781530033881